Belongs to :

Lenny Nader

Collecting
Barber Bottles

Pictorial Price Guide
With History

Richard Holiner

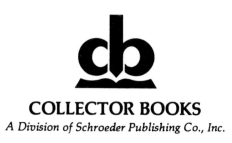

COLLECTOR BOOKS
A Division of Schroeder Publishing Co., Inc.

Additional copies of this book may be ordered from:

Collector Books
P.O. Box 3009
Paducah, KY 42001

@$24.95 Add $1.00 for postage and handling.

Copyright: Richard Holiner, 1986

Foreword

Barbering and shaving collectibles are highly sought by collectors today. Barber bottles, shaving mugs, fancy straight and safety razors, even furnishings such as barber poles and chairs are popular. Some collectors specialize in one segment of the collecting field. Many have general collections. A few have recreated an entire interior of a barber shop within their home complete with backbar, chairs, pole and all accoutrements. A typical barber bottle collector could be someone wishing to collect any bottle pattern not already in his possession, with some collections numbering several hundred different examples. Another might be a collector of a particular type of Art Glass, purchasing barber bottles in that pattern and not really interested in barber bottle collecting. A third example of a barber bottle collector might be one that wishes to obtain a half dozen different colorful barber bottles to decorate his bathroom.

There are several comprehensive books available concerned with collecting shaving mugs and straight razors. But until now, very little has been produced concerned with the many varied and colorful patterns of barber bottles. This book fills that void.

The key to intelligent collecting decisions lies with obtaining accurate information on the history, variety of patterns and the values of a particular collectible. The beginning, advanced and potential collector of barber bottles will find this book most informative.

Dick Holiner has left nothing to the imagination. The extensive color illustrations accurately portray the beauty of the art glass and the variety of shapes. The text is accurate and succinct, with the photo captions adding additional information on each particular bottle pattern.

Having auctioned many hundreds of barber bottles over the last few years, I feel that I am qualified to state that the prices reflected in this book are quite accurate with true market. Pricing is always the most difficult and controversial aspect of a collectable guide. This accuracy of pricing is the final product of diligent research and meticulous recordkeeping by this experienced author—Dick Holiner.

This specialty reference book will have a prominent position in my library, as I am certain I will refer to it often.

Robert A. Doyle
Auctioneers & Appraisers
Fishkill, NY

This book is dedicated to Walter F. Sill, Jr., my good friend and partner.

A Special Thanks to the Following List of Contributors:

Mr. and Mrs. Bird Lanham, Madisonville, Kentucky
Mr. and Mrs. Ralph Thyng, Evansville, Indiana
Mr. Val Everson, Brandford, Connecticut
Mr. Edward Leach, Patterson, New Jersey
Robert Doyle, Doyle Auctioneers, Fishkill, New York
Mr. Water F. Sill, Jr., Nashville, Tennessee
Mr. Kenny Drew, "The Pack Rat," Evansville, Indiana
Mr. Tony Gugliotti, Wolcott, Connecticut

Introduction

From around the 1870's until the turn of the century, many barbers mixed their own tonics and facial splashes, such as Witch Hazel and Bay Rum. When the pure food and drug act of 1906 restricted the use of alcohol-based substances in unlabeled and re-fillable containers, barber bottles for the most part were no longer used for their original purpose and were taken out of service.

The beauty and varied styles of these bottles, in my opinion, is the reason that so many have survived and are in collections today. In their heyday, barber shops were visited by business men on a more regular basis than today. Along with the trims, manicuring etc., much good fellowship and conversation took place.

As barbers took pride in their shops, their bottles became increasingly more distinctive and personalized. Bottles, usually used in pairs, were ordered for the better customers and used with their own special mixture. These bottles contained shampoos, hair tonics and facial toners. Later barbers would refill bottles from commercial containers, holding up to twenty-five gallons, which they purchased from their salesman or distributor.

With the invention of the safety razor, men started shaving at home more often, using stylized bottles of their own or ones they purchased from the barber shops they used to frequent so often.

Many bottles were made and imported from Europe, mainly from Bohemia (Poland and Hungary) and Czechoslovakia. Some other countries were Austria, Germany, Italy, Belgium, France and England. Very few of these bottles were marked, neither were those made in this country.

Some of the well known companies in the United States were: The Boston and Sandwich Glass Company, New England Glass Works and Hobbs, Brokunier and Company. Later contributors were the Fostoria Glass Company and Fenton Glass Works. T. White Hall Tatum Glass Company made bottles for Koken and Kochs, two of the most popular barber supply houses. Some of the most interesting barber bottles for functional use were still being made during the 1920's.

Most of the earliest bottles were made of lighter glass, were hand blown and had exposed or improved pontils. Exposed pontils are rough, unfinished and came from using iron rods with glass tips from which the bottle was broken after it was blown. Improved pontils came as a result of using iron rods with a flared tip and when pressed against the bottom of the bottle, produced a finished indentation. Early bottles were also cut and pressed. Bottles were both bottom and top blown, but most of the bottles made after the turn of the century were mould blown. Recent mould blown bottles will show the mould line on the lip of the bottle. Older bottles had the lip applied after the bottle was blown. Other age factors to look for are honest bottom ware and a cork that shows age and is frozen to the inside neck of the bottle. Bubbles and irregularities in the glass are other tell-tale age signs.

Many art glass styles of the day were also made for barber use. Fancy pressed and cut glass was desirable. Milk glass was popular because the white opaque background showed personal names, product identification and decoration so well. Enameled and colored bottles were also in demand because they were showy—especially the Mary Gregory styles using young boys and girls in white enameled scenes.

Collectors today seem to favor amethyst, cranberry and cobalt blue, although emerald greens and dark ambers are also popular. Various shades of red are high on the list but hard to find. Gold was needed to get red in glass. Personalized milk glass or bottles with labels under glass overlays are among the most sought after by advanced collectors, along with miniatures. Labels under glass overlays did not last long. They cracked easily, also the alcohol-based ingredients would run down between the bottle and label, stain and cause the glass overlay to fall off. Matching glass waste bowls are very desirable, but few survived and are seldom seen.* Another very rare bottle is made of papier mache built up over the glass to resemble wood bark. It also has a label under glass overlay.

* Refer to partially reproduced Kochs catalog in back of this book.

The most common styles seen are Opaline-deco style (page 97); Hobnail, probably the most popular style in its time (page 62); round bulbous base, short to long straight neck, (page 36 and 86) round bulbous base, lady leg neck (page 9).

Occasionally you will see bottles that have an unusual shape or some other feature that is not characteristic of most barber bottles. Most were not originally meant for tonic or facial splashes, but adapted to that use; some examples are shown on page 94. Some of the more common clear glass bottles were under multiple listings in barber supply catalogs and meant for use in both barber shops and restaurants. Manufacturers and distributors received orders from time to time for those not in stock and special orders for unusual colors or shades. Bottles supplied in some cases were originally meant for the art glass market; ornamental vases are one example (page 25 and 95). These bottles had glass closures with ground inside necks, ground and polished tops or very wide top openings that were not practical for the average cork and "squirt" closure. Around the turn of the century and even before in unpopulated areas, salesmen and distributors were not too accessible, so barbers at times used what was available—maybe a vase from home that had a functional shape, or some bottle picked up at the general store.

Bottle heights in this book do not include the metal (pewter, Britiania) or porcelain "squirt" closures. Cork was used to give the closures a tight fit and not allow excess liquid to run out. Ball and crown spouts were used on the more expensive essences to keep the alcohol-based substances from evaporating.

A good number of the bottles found will still have sediment and evaporation lines inside. You probably will want to clean this out, especially in the lighter colored or clearer bottles. The most effective way I have found is to break up an Efferdent tablet, using warm or hot water. Let the ingredients complete the bubbling action, than rinse with clean water. If the dirt still persists, use Drano, but let me caution you to be careful— this is a powerful substance and directions on the can should be followed using only cold water. Drano creates heat as it works. I have never used acid, but some say that certain types will clear up "sick" bottles. The reason is obvious why I cannot recommend this dangerous substance.

Before cleaning a bottle, if it has a cork, remove it. If it is frozen to the inside neck of the bottle, use a thin bladed knife inserted between the glass and cork. Slowly work it around until the cork is free, then put something like a dental tool or button hook down through the hole in the cork and slowly work it out. Be careful as older cork is usually brittle.

My pricing spread indicates where the price of each bottle usually will be and should be considered a fair retail price, the lower figure represents wholesale to low retail. Those bottles which have been personalized, those having labels under glass overlays, fine enameled colored glass and cut glass bottles of rare and exceptional quality will bring higher prices especially at better auctions.

Auctions that specialize in barber shop memorabilia and general or estate auctions that advertise numerous quality bottles coming up for sale are probably the truest barometer of current prices and values. These auctions attract knowledgeable dealers and collectors. Consequently, bidding is usually active, with dealers taking bottles to wholesale, and serious or advanced collectors bidding higher for the most desirable pieces.

Flea markets, small antique stores and malls are where most bargains are found but for the most part, quality bottles which have been collectable for around fifty years are in collections and hard to find. The bottles in my collection and those borrowed for use in this book are from the middle west and east coast. The prices are reflective of those areas. Nowhere else in the United States were barber shops in such profusion, before and around the turn of the century, as on the east coast. Today the number of collectors in this area is also great because of the availability of barber shop antiques.

Specialized auction houses, such as Doyles in Fishkill, New York, take many phone and mail bids from around the country at each of their auctions. For this and the above mentioned reasons, I feel that this area sets pricing standards.

Matched pair, 8″ high, exposed pontils, rolled lips, iridescent green, gilted and enameled Art Nouveau style.

Matched pair, 7½″ high, sheared lips, exposed pontils, cobalt blue enameled floral design, Art Nouveau style.

Matched pair of cobalt blue and amethyst, 7¾″ high, exposed pontils, rolled lips, enameled floral design.

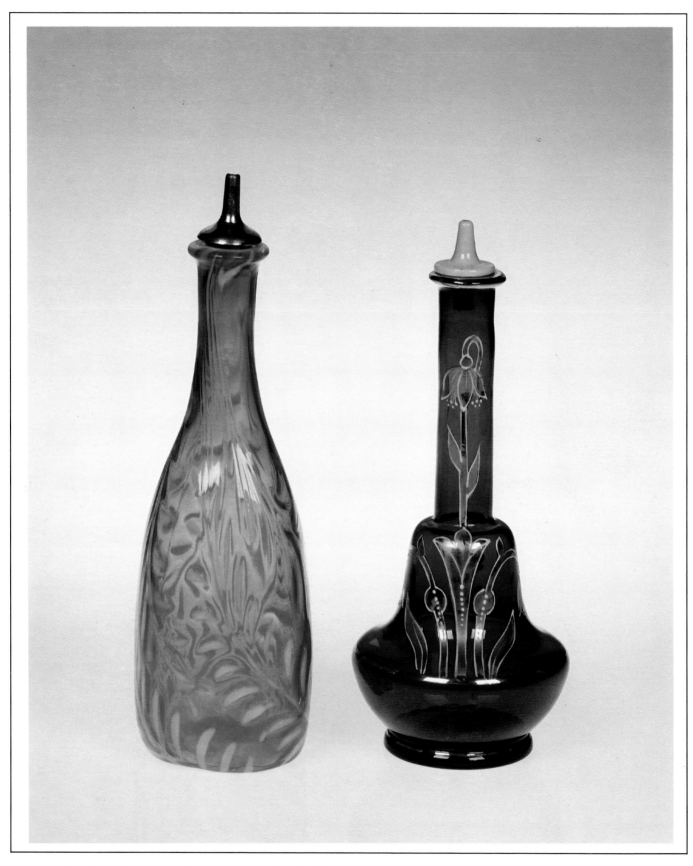

Left: opalized cranberry fern design, 8¼″ high, rolled lip. **Right:** amethyst enameled floral design Art Nouveau style, 7¾″ high, exposed pontil, rolled lip.

Matched pair amethyst, 8″ high, exposed pontils, rolled lips, enameled Mary Gregory style.

Matched pair amethyst, 8¼″ high, exposed pontils, rolled lips, enameled Mary Gregory style.

Matched pair green, 8″ high, exposed pontils, rolled lips, enameled Mary Gregory style.

Limegreen, 8″ high, exposed pontil, rolled lip, enameled Mary Gregory style.

Matched pair of cobalt blue, 8⅜″ high, exposed pontils, rolled lips, enameled Mary Gregory style.

Matched pair cranberry, 9½″ high, sheared lips, top blown, enameled Mary Gregory style.

Three T. White Hall Tatum, hand painted and personalized milk glass, 9¾″ high, screw-on tops. This style of personalized milk glass is at the top of the list of most advanced collectors.

Matched pair, 10″ high, hand painted milk glass. I have seen this same bottle but smaller with original factory label for ginger ale, probably used for other similar products.

Hand Painted Milk Glass with Floral Design and Product Identification

From Left: 8¾″ high, rolled lip, "Seafoam" is very faint; 8¾″ high, rolled lip, toilet water; 8¾″ high, name of tonic or facial splash has been ground off; 9¼″ high, rolled lip, Bay Rum. This style of bottle is considered very desirable by most advanced collectors.

Matched pair hand painted milk glass, 9″ high, rolled lips. These bottles were offered for sale by Kochs Barber Supply Company. Refer to partially reproduced Koch's catalog in back of this book. Considered very desirable by most advanced collectors.

Left: blue milk glass with label under glass overlay, 8¾″ high, rolled lip. The price of bottles with labels under glass overlays depends on condition of label and glass overlay. **Right:** Hand painted milk glass, 9″ high, rolled lip.

Left: pair of clear and milk glass dresser bottles, 8¼″ & 8½″ high. **Center:** milk glass dresser bottle, 6¾″ high, exposed pontil. **Right:** milk glass Koken Barber Supply bottle, 8″ high.

Pair of white and black milk glass, 7¾″ & 8¼″ high, rolled lips. The white is Koken Barber Supply, the black is Art Deco style and rare.

Left: Bristol glass, hand painted fox and hound scene, 7½″ high, exposed pontil, sheared lip. **Right:** hand painted milk glass with rose and leaf design, 6¾″ high, rolled lip.

Left: blue mellon sided, 8⅛″ high, rolled lip. **Top center:** milk glass Koken Barber Supply, 7½″ high, rolled lip. **Bottom center:** French, cobalt blue enameled floral design, 8⅜″ high, sheared lip, approximately 100 years old, very unusual shape. **Right:** light blue hand painted and enameled floral design, 7⅛″ high, exposed pontil. There was a pair of these originally, one was broken. They were used in a barber shop in Newport, Kentucky, for years. Both bottles had ground inside necks and glass stoppers. Not originally made for tonic, but adapted to that use.

Matched pair opalized cranberry splatter, 8″ high, improved pontil. These bottles are in many collections, listed as barber bottles in most auctions. I am not saying that they were not used by barbers, but the fact that the tops are ground and polished, the bottoms overly large and unwieldly, indicates to me that they were probably originally meant for the art glass market.

Left: opalized cranberry splatter, 10″ high, sheared lip, very unusual shape. Pewter spout unscrews to expose pouring vents. **Right:** opalized cranberry splatter, 8¼″ high, rolled lip, square base.

Opalized cranberry splatter, 8½″ high, rolled lip, square base.

Opalized green splatter, 7½″ high, exposed pontil, rolled lip.

Cranberry, 8″ high, exposed pontil, sheared lip, enameled floral design, bell shape.

Venetian glass, 8½″ high, exposed pontil. Has original McKesson Bay Rum label, this bottle shows good bottom ware and has a frozen cork and spout. This style was also produced later.

Blue and purple art glass, Lotz style, probably French, 7⅜″ high, sheared lip.

Enameled and hand painted, 8″ high, exposed pontil, sheared lip.

Ruby cut to clear Bohemian style, 8⅜″ high.

Ruby cut to clear Bohemian style, 9½″ high, rolled lip, square base, grape vine design.

Amethyst, 7″ high, sheared lip, enameled floral design. I have seen this style of bottle used as a whiskey decanter. The opening at the top is very wide at 1¾₁₆″. The cork and perfectly fitted brass spout are frozen to the inside neck, so I feel this was used as a tonic bottle.

Matched pair amethyst, 8″ high, sheared lips, dot and floral design.

Matched set of four — two in green, two in amethyst, 8″ high, exposed pontils, sheared lips, enemeled dot and floral design with brown bands.

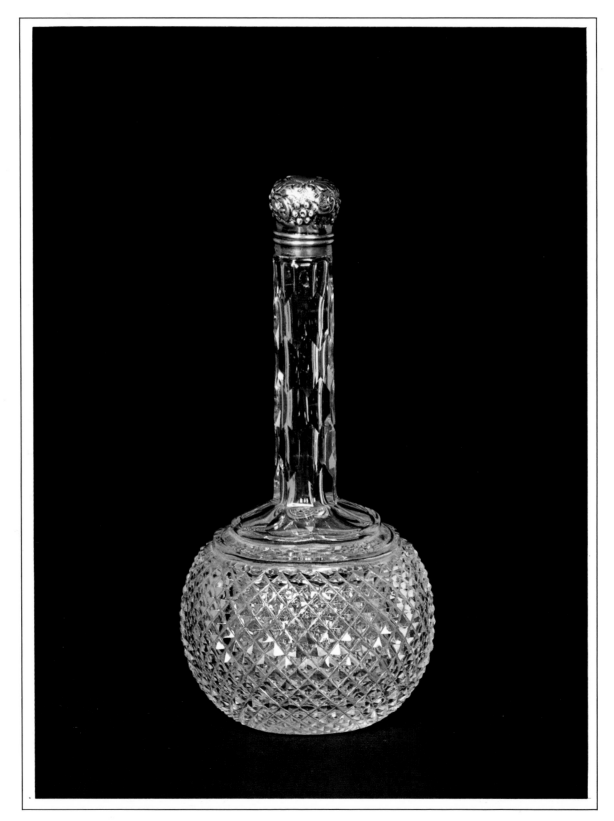

Dresser bottle, cut crystal, ground bottom with sterling top, 7¾″ high. A fine quality bottle from the collection of Val Everson, Brandford, Connecticut.

Left: frosted stars and stripes, 8¼″ high, rolled lip. **Right:** dresser bottle, fancy cut, ground and etched decanter style, 8½″ high.

Left: dresser bottle, heavy crystal or flint glass, etched with sterling top, "Hawks" stamped on bottom, 7″ high, rolled lip. **Right:** crystal, New England glass, 7½″ high, improved pontil.

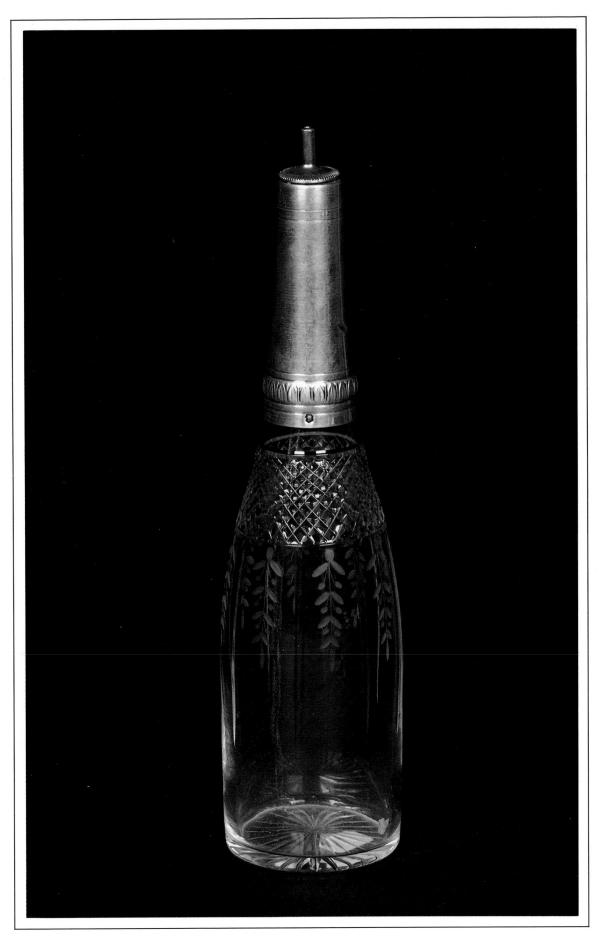

Dresser bottle, cut and etched with hallmarked silver top, 8¾″ high.

Left: pressed star burst design, 6¾″ high, rolled lip.
Right: pressed diamond design, 7¼″ high, rolled lip.

Matched set of fancy dresser bottles, 6¼″ high.

42

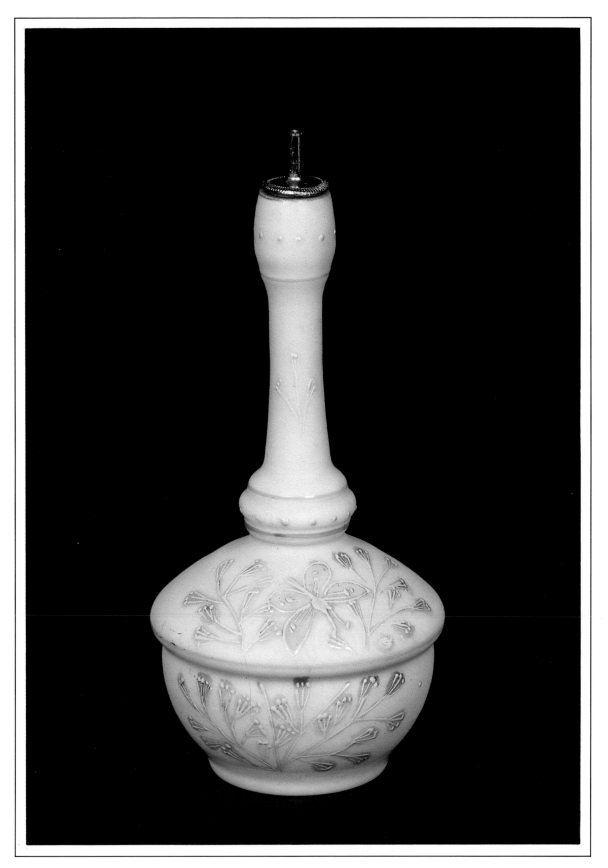

Bristol glass dresser bottle, 7¼″ high, sheared lip, enameled floral and butterfly design.

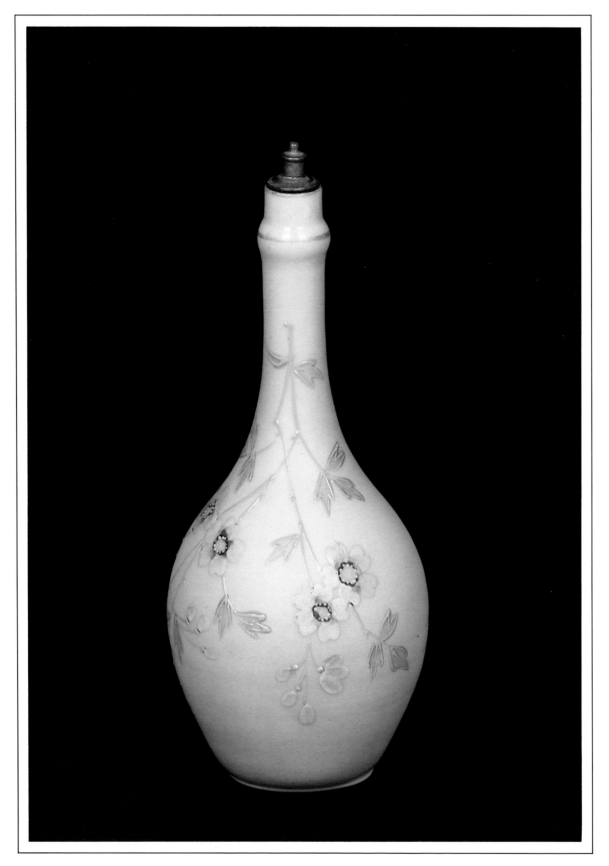

Pink Bristol glass dresser bottle, 7¼″ high, exposed pontil, sheared lip, enameled floral design.

Left: aqua blue, 6¼″ high, rolled lip. **Right:** ruby red, cut and ground dresser bottle, 6¾″ high, improved pontil.

Teal blue, 7½″ high, improved pontil, sheared lip, enameled floral design.

Cobalt blue enameled miniature, 5½″ high, exposed pontil, rolled lip. This is a true miniature and generally was used to hold "Brilliantine", a popular hair tonic of the time. Rare.

Miniature brilliantine bottle, pressed ruby glass, 4″ high. Rare.

Left: teal blue mellon sided coin spot, 8⅜″ high, rolled lip. **Right:** bell shaped Bristol glass, hand painted and enameled light blue, 7½″ high, improved pontil, sheared lip. Refer to partially reproduced Koch's catalog in the back of this book.

Left: light amber enameled Art Nouveau design, 8⅜″ high, exposed pontil, rolled lip. Refer to partially reproduced Koch's catalog (waste bowls) in the back of this book. **Right:** apple green enameled dot and daisy design, 8½″ high, exposed pontil, rolled lip.

Pair of amethyst and light blue, 7¾″ & 7⅞″ high, exposed pontils, rolled lips, enameled floral design.

Amethyst, 8″ high, exposed pontil, rolled lip, enameled dot and daisy design.

Amethyst, 7¾″ high, exposed pontil, rolled lip, enameled floral design.

Opalized cranberry, melon sided coin spot, 8¼″ high, rolled lip. Unusually long neck for this style.

Iridescent amber, 8″ high, exposed pontil, rolled lip, enameled floral design, Art Nouveau style. Refer to partially reproduced Koch's catalog in the back of this book.

Amethyst, 8″ high, rolled lip, exposed pontil. Enameled "Vegederma" a brand of hair tonic, Art Nouveau style. Refer to partially reproduced Koch's catalog in back of this book.

Matched pair amethyst, 7¾″ high, exposed pontils, rolled lips, enameled "De Vrys," "Exquise Tonique". This was a barber supply company in Evansville, Indiana.

Pair of light blue and cobalt blue, 7½″ high, exposed pontils, sheared and rolled lips, enameled daisy and fleur-de-lis designs.

Amber, 8¾″ high, rolled lip, enameled dot and floral design.

Left: multi-colored venetian glass, 8⅝″ high, exposed pontil. **Center:** Fenton art glass, 8¼″ high, rolled lip. Notice original factory label, also stamped on bottom. **Right:** very light blue enameled floral design, 8″ high, rolled lip. These bottles are examples that were made after World War II.

Amberina hobnail, 6¾″ high, improved pontil, rolled lip. Rare in this color.

Pair of satin finish amethyst and opalized blue hobnail, 7″ & 6¾″ high, improved pontils, rolled lips.

Matched pair vaseline and light blue hobnail, 7⅛″ high, improved pontils, rolled lips.

Pair of opalized blue hobnail, 7⅜″ & 8″ high, exposed pontils, rolled lips.

Matched pair amethyst, 7½″ high, rolled lips.

Matched pair vaseline hobnail, 7″ high, improved pontils, rolled lips.

Matched pair amber hobnail, 7¼″ high, improved pontils, rolled lips.

Matched pair cranberry hobnail, 7″ high, improved pontils, rolled lips.

Pair of opalized cranberry hobnail, 7″ high, improved pontils, rolled lips.

Pair of clear opalized hobnail, 7″ and 8″ high, improved pontils, rolled lips.

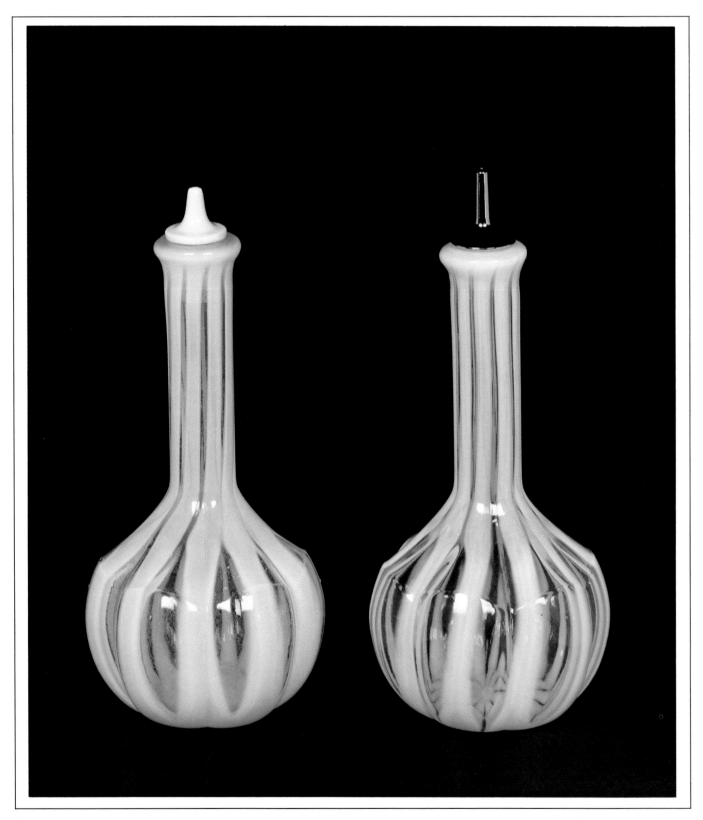

Matched pair opalized yellow green melon sided, 7½″ high, rolled lips.

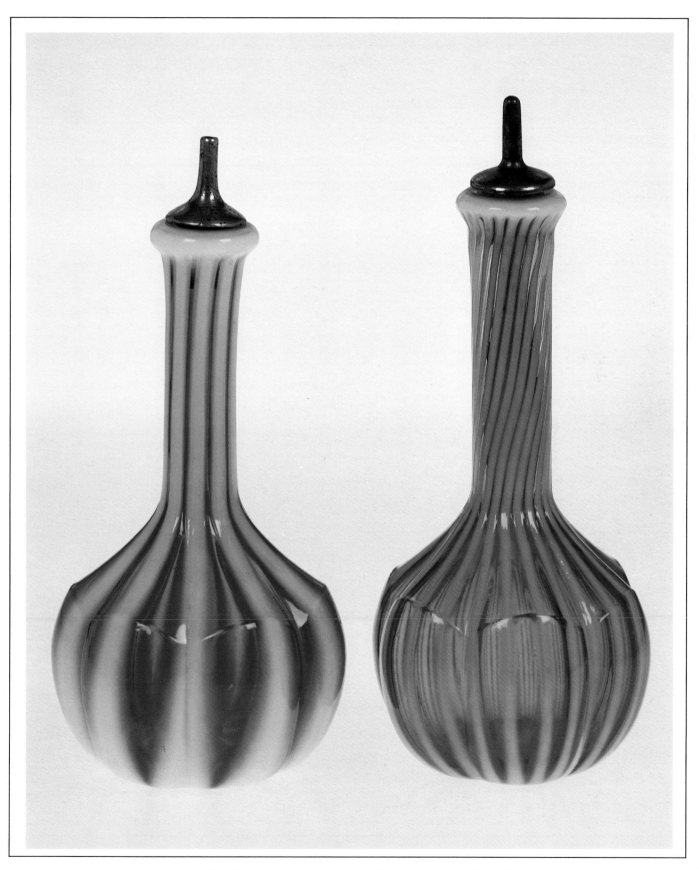

Pair of opalized cranberry melon sided, 7⅛″ & 7½″ high, rolled lips.

Left: teal blue enameled Persian design, 6⅞″ high, exposed pontil, sheared lip. **Right:** melon sided satin finish opalized cranberry, 7″ high, rolled lip.

Left: lime green Persian design, 6½" high, exposed pontil, sheared lip. **Right:** cobalt blue dot and fleur-de-lis design, 6⅝" high, exposed pontil, sheared lip.

Left: opalized cranberry melon sided fern design, 7″ high, rolled lip. **Right:** emerald green melon sided coin spot, 7″ high, rolled lip.

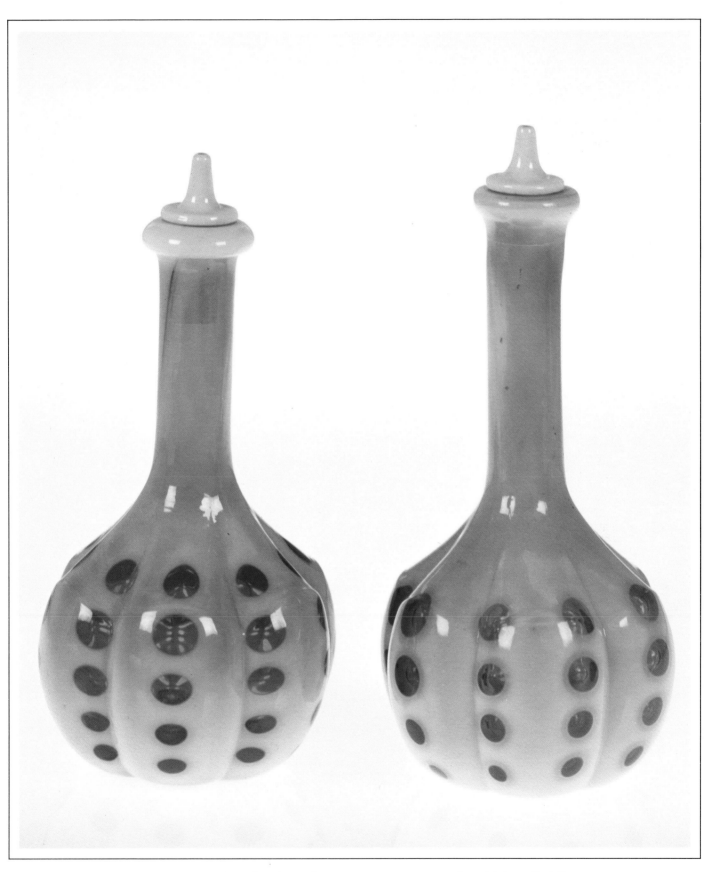

Matched pair of opalized cranberry coin spot, 6¾″ and 7″ high, rolled lips.

Opalized blue "stars and stripes" design, 7″ high, rolled lip, improved pontil.

Left: opalized blue spanish lace, 7″ high, rolled lip, improved pontil. **Right:** opalized cranberry swirl, 7″ high, rolled lip, improved pontil.

Left: opalized pale green daisy and fern design, 7″ high, rolled lip. **Right:** satin finish opalized cranberry daisy and fern design, 7″ high, rolled lip.

Left: matched set melon sided cranberry, 7¼″ high, rolled lips. **Right:** matched set thumb print cranberry, 7¼″ high, rolled lips.

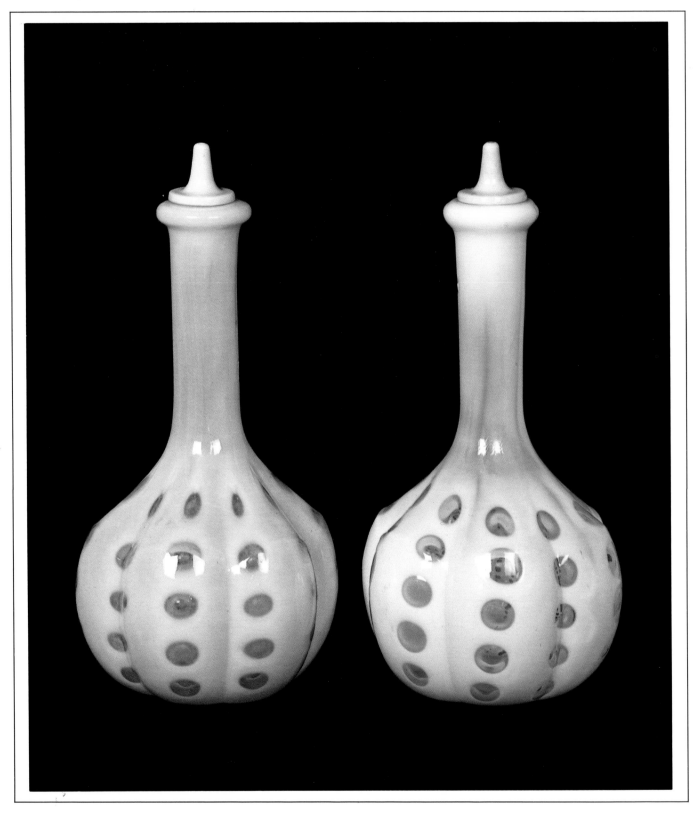

Matched pair clear opalized coin spot, 7″ high, rolled lips.

Left: cobalt blue enameled floral design, 7″ high, exposed pontil, sheared lip. **Right:** light blue opalized coin spot, 6½″ high, rolled lip.

Pair of opalized blue and cranberry spanish lace, 7¼″ & 7″ high, improved pontils, rolled lips.

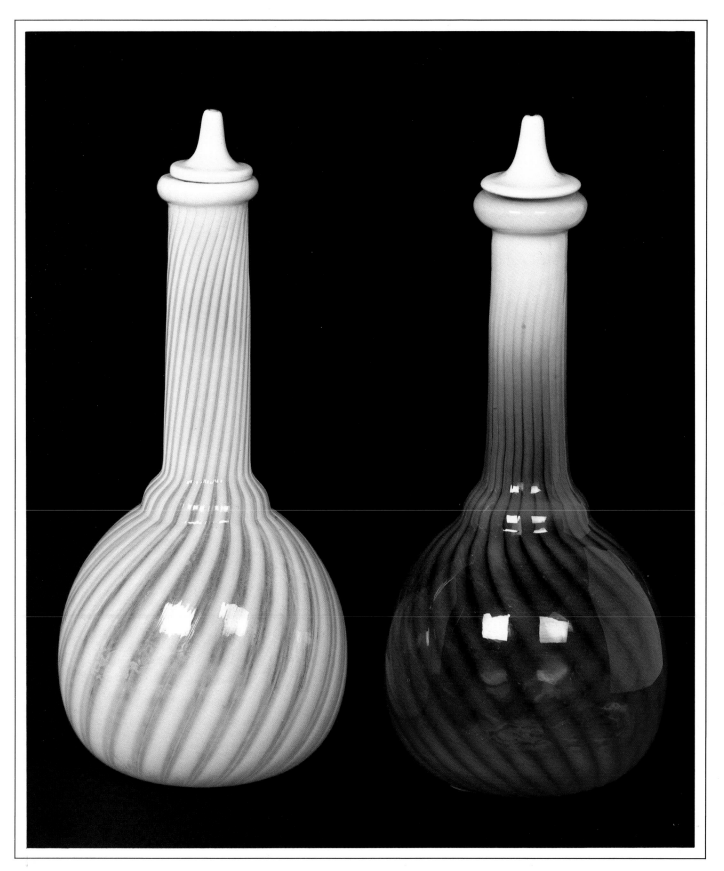

Pair of opalized clear and cranberry swirl, 7″ high, improved pontils, rolled lips.

Matched pair amethyst and cobalt blue, 7⅛″ high, exposed pontils, rolled lips, enameled and painted daisy and leaf design.

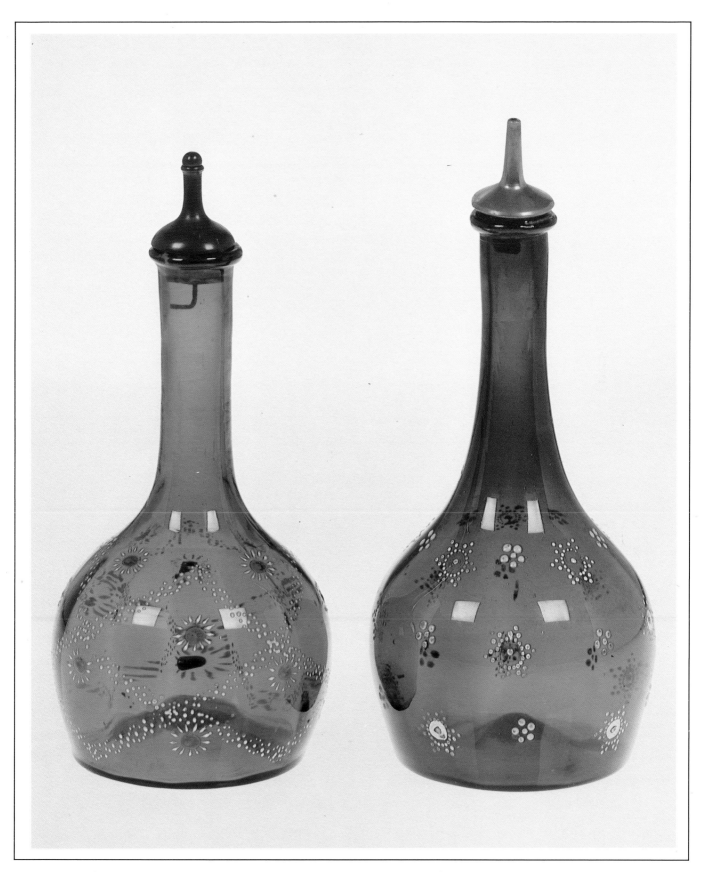

Pair of dark and emerald green, 6⅝″ & 7″ high, exposed pontils, rolled lips, enameled dot and daisy design.

Pair of amethyst and light blue, 6⅝″ & 6⅞″ high, exposed pontils, sheared and rolled lips, enameled daisy design.

Pair of amethyst, 6⅜″ & 7¼″ high, exposed pontils, rolled and sheared lips, enameled floral designs.

Pair of amethyst and green, 6⅞" high, exposed pontils, sheared lips, enameled dot and floral design.

Matched pair light blue and amethyst, 7″ high, exposed pontils, sheared lips, enameled dot and floral design.

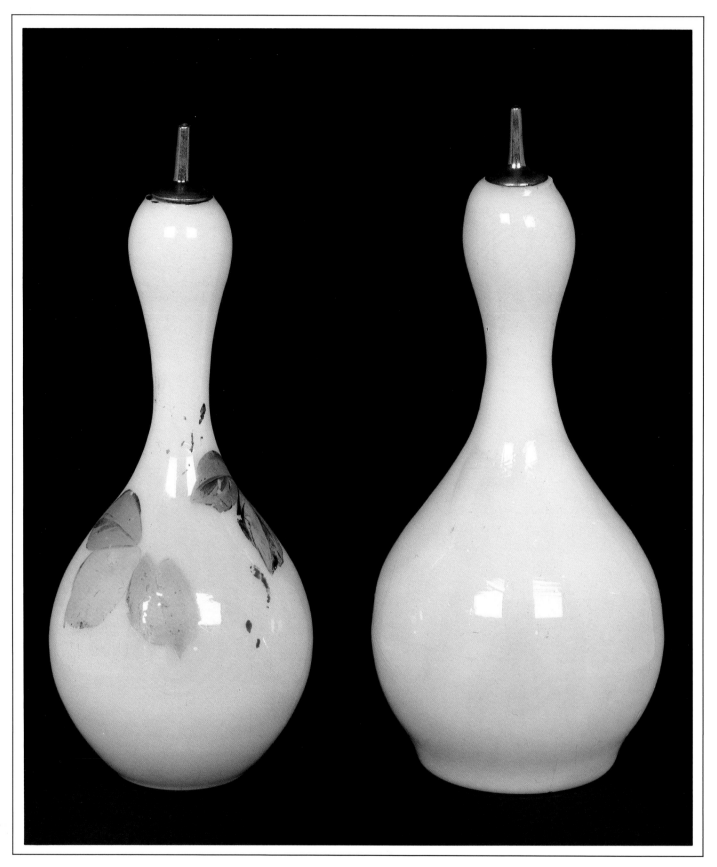

Pair of Bristol glass, 7¼" & 7¾" high, hand painted leaf and floral design.

Old green glass covered in wicker, 5½″ high. This is unusual, came out of a large collection and is known to have been used by a barber. The cork is frozen to inside neck, the spout is two-piece and has a gilted finish.

Avon 1963 Close Harmony (barber bottle). Was available in spicy and original aftershave, also Vigorate and after-shower cologne, screw on cap, 6½″ high.

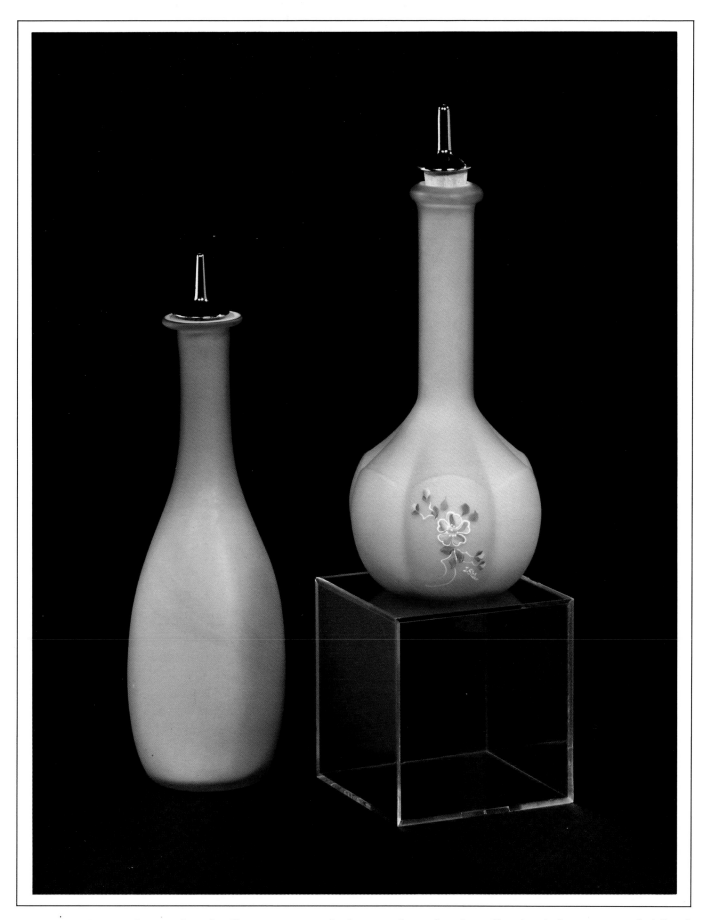

Pair of cased satin glass pink and yellow, 7½″ & 8⅝″ high, recently made. The yellow bottle has an enameled floral design and is signed.

Group of bottles not originally made as a barber bottles, but converted to that use.

Left: porcelain with cobalt blue overlay, made in Austria and used by a barber in Axtell, Nebraska, for many years, 7″ high. **Center:** cobalt blue with enameled floral design, 8¼″ high, rolled lip. The inside neck of this bottle is ground and originally had a glass stopper. **Right:** Bristol glass hand painted and enameled, 6½″ high, exposed pontil. This bottle originally had a flared lip, which was ground off (probably because it was chipped or broken) and a spout was added.

Left: highly decorated (enameled) Bristol glass, 7⅞″ high. **Right:** opalized cranberry swirl, 8″ high, improved pontil, sheared lip. Both of these particular bottles, although not made originally as barber bottles, are known to have been used in a barber shop. The cranberry swirl came from Crestview, Ohio.

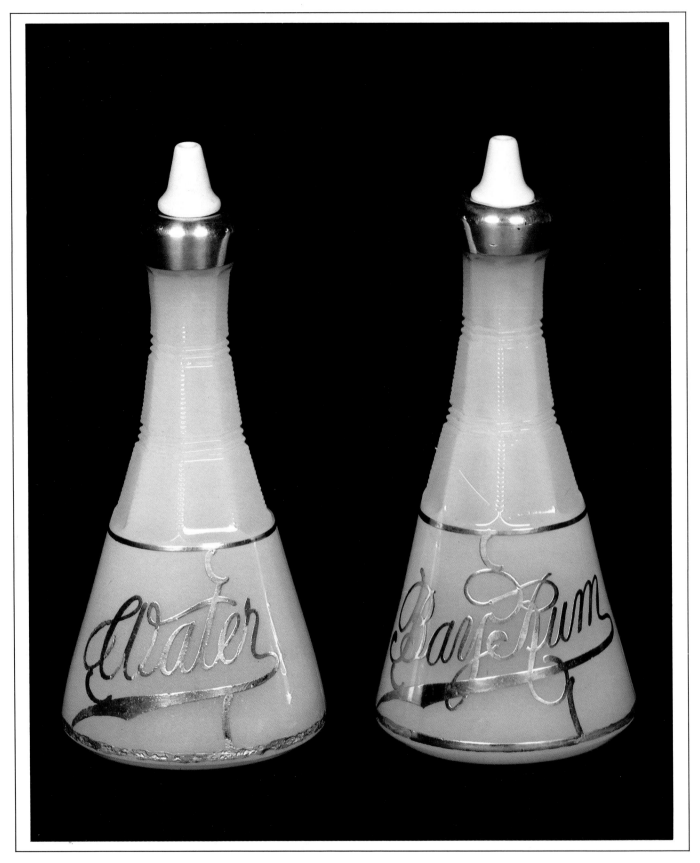

Matched pair opaline, 7″ high, silver overlay identification and caps, deco style.

Set of opaline with stenciled identification and antiseptic container, 6¾″ high.

Set of opaline hand painted identification with antiseptic jar, 7″ high.

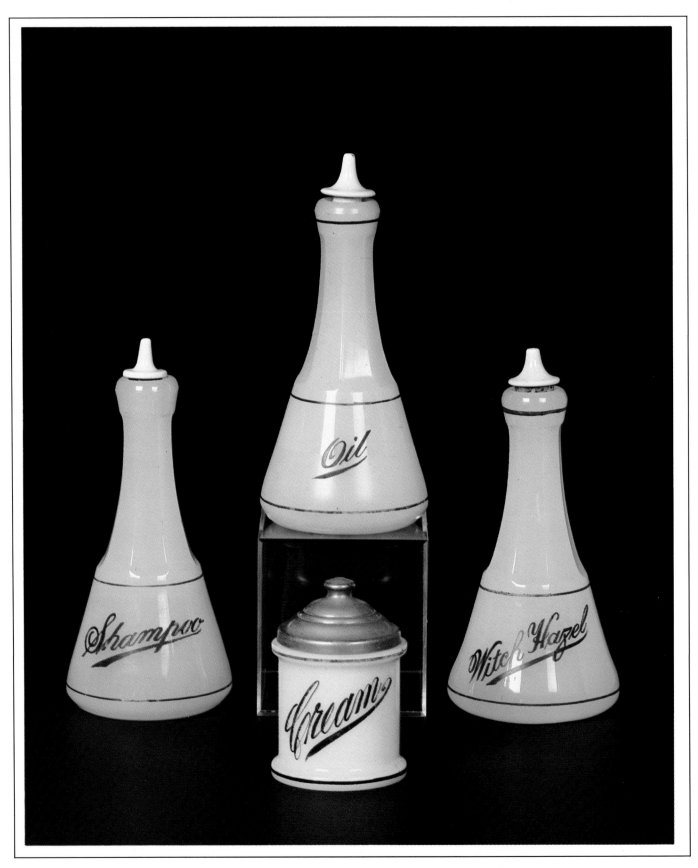

Set of opaline with hand painted identification and matching créme jar, 7″ high.

Set of three Wapler Barber Supply House bottles. Company was located in New York, 7″ to 7⅜″ high, rolled lips.

Group of commercial bottles, were available both retail and in barber shops, 7¼″ to 8½″ high.

Matched pair, label under glass overlay, 7¾" high. Commercial variety, but still desirable because of label under glass overlay.

Three turn-of-the-century company-packaged hair tonic bottles, 7½″ to 8¾″ high. Heights include original stoppers. These bottles could be purchased in retail outlets or barber shops.

Pair of cobalt blue Ayer's hair vigor bottles, 7½″ high. The stopper on one bottle is exposed to show the unusual glass dauber, which is recessed in the cork.

From left: Colgate commercial toilet water, 6½″ high; Palmer commercial toilet water from Red Lodge, Montana, 7″ high; Kickapoo Sage commercial hair tonic, Kickapoo Indiana Medicine Company, 5½″ high; Demond brand commercial hair oil, 7¼″ high. This old bottle and old label have been married, but correctly.

Pair of unusually shaped green and amber company packaged facial splash bottles, 9¼″ & 9½″ high. The green bottle is early 1800s and British. The amber bottle is this century and from Georgetown, St. Vincent Island in the Carribean.

Group of three commercial bay rum bottles, 6½″ to 9⅜″ high. Company: McKesson, Larkin and Georgetown, St. Vincent Island in the Carribean, covered with wicker.

Left: Sportsmans shaving lotion, made in 1955 for Fathers Day, mugs were also available, 5⅜″ high. **Center:** amber, this bottle originally had a label under glass overlay, 7⅛″ high. With label and glass overlay intact, price would be much higher. **Right:** T. White Hall Tatum commercial Bay Rum, 7″ high.

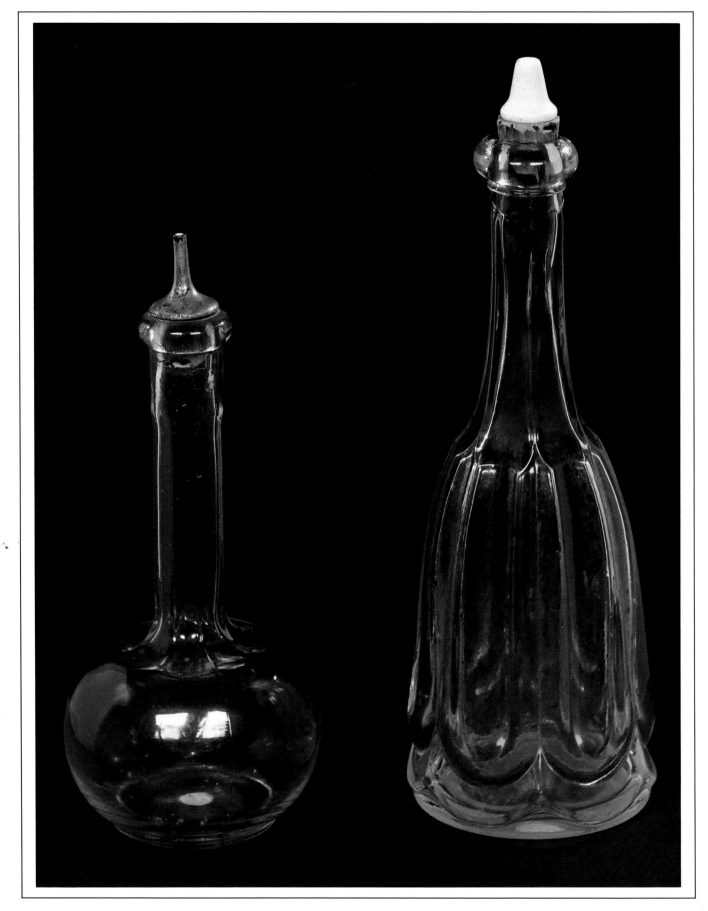

Pair of clear pressed glass, 7⅜″ and 9⅝″ high. The larger of the two is heavy flint glass, with a ground, unpolished bottom. Was also used as a whiskey decanter, with a glass stopper.

Group of clear pressed glass, 7″ to 8¾″ high. These bottles were generally used in barber shops, but were also used in restaurants for ketchup, vinegar etc.

Group of clear pressed glass, 6″ to 6¾″ high, rolled and sheared lips. These bottles were in catalogs under multiple listings. They were generally used in restaurants and homes as vinegar, oil and condiment cruets, but were also used as barber bottles. Restaurants had to use clear bottles so customers could see the contents.

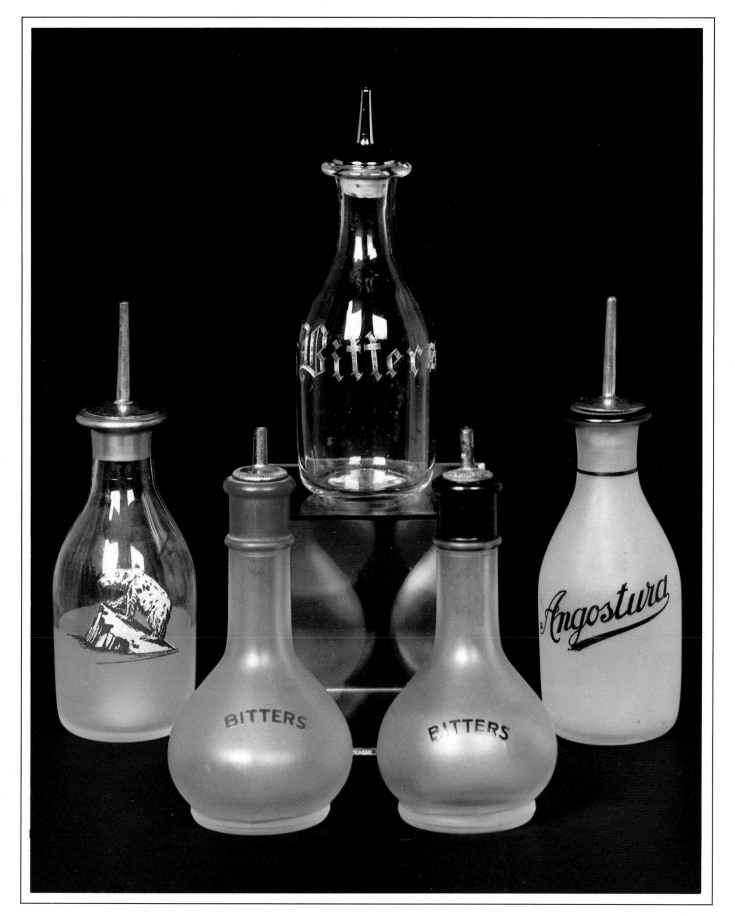

Group of bitters bottles, 5″ to 5¼″ high. These were tavern and saloon bottles used on back bars. They were under multi-listing and were used occasionally in barber shops.

Group of three barber supply house bottles with raised lettering, 7¼″ to 10½″ high. The two smaller bottles are De Vrys, Evansville, Indiana. The larger is Atlantic, Atlanta, Georgia.

Matched pair of T. White Hall Tatum personalized hand painted milk glass, 9¾" high, screw on cap. Frank Lambert was one of the founding fathers of Lambertsville, New Jersey. From the collection of Edward Leach, Patterson, New Jersey.

Clear glass with label under glass overlay, 9¼" high. This particular bottle is damaged and would be much higher if intact.

Left: clear opalized hobnail, 7″ high, exposed pontil, rolled lip. **Left center:** hand painted milk glass, 7½″ high, exposed pontil, rolled lip. **Right center:** milk glass, Koken style, 7¾″ high, rolled lip. **Right:** clear opalized "stars & stripes", 7″ high, rolled lip.

Top row: matched pair of Art glass, Lotz, France, 7½″ high, sheared lips. **Bottom row:** left: emerald green toilet water, "Penslar", 7¼″ high. **Center:** cobalt blue; Mary Gregory style enameled "toilet water", Windmill design, 8″ high, exposed pontil, rolled lip. This design rare in Mary Gregory; another has a Gristmill. **Right:** pressed, ruby flash, 6¾″ high, rolled lip.

Imported Glassware—Original and Exclusive Designs

NOTHING adds more to the attractiveness of the barber shop than the glassware which is used upon the shelf of the mirror case. If the bottles containing the toilet preparations, the vases for shaving paper, etc., are of a neat and attractive style the customer's impression is a favorable one. Our line of Bohemian Glassware is strictly modern and includes exclusive and novel designs at prices which will be found very moderate.

No. 76. Shaving Paper Vase
Imperial red with rich gold decoration.
Matches No. 76 bottles.
Each............................$2.25

No. 785. Shaving Paper Vase
White opaque glass, handsomely decorated.
Matches No. 16 bottles
Each............................85c

No. 73. Shaving Paper Vase
Clear glass with decoration in white
enamel relief.
Matches No. 73 bottles.
Each............................$1.15

No. 78. Shaving Paper Vase
Clear frosted glass.
Matches No. 78 bottles. A very striking
design and extremely attractive.
Each............................$1.25

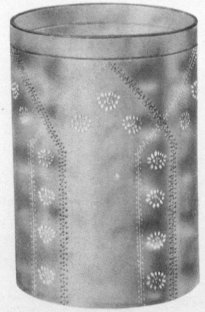

No. 25. Shaving Paper Vase
Matches No. 81 bottles and
No. 25 bowls.
Each............................90c

No. 74. Shaving Paper Vase
Clear glass with flower decoration
in striking colors.
Matches No. 74 bottles.
Each............................$1.15

Catalog reprint from *Barbers Supplies*, Theo Koch and Son, New York, catalog #15, 1915.

Imported Glassware—Original and Exclusive Designs

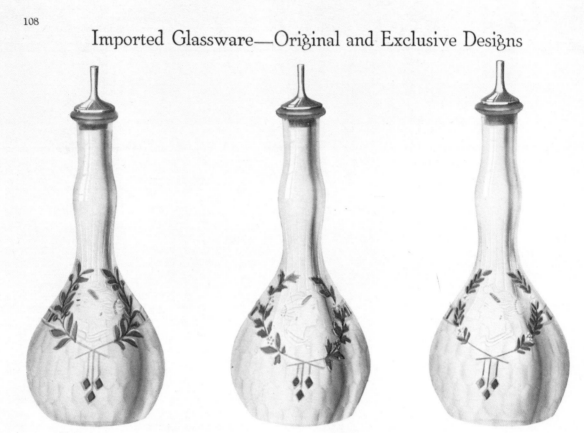

Made of clear glass with different floral decoration. Heads in white-enamel relief on each of the three bottles constituting a set.

No. 73. Stand Bottles, each . . . . 45c   No. 73. Bowls to match, each 50c

No. 73. Shaving Paper Vases to match, each $1.15

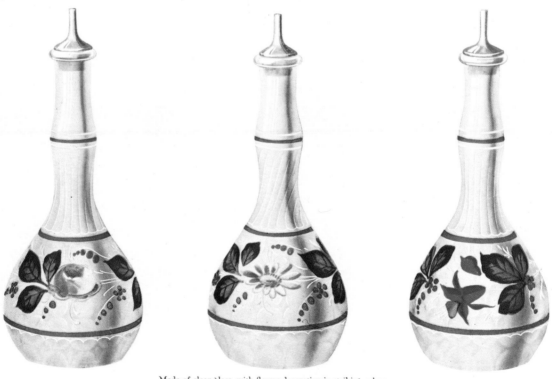

Made of clear glass, with flower decoration in striking colors.

No. 74. Stand Bottles, each . . . . 45c   No. 74. Bowls to match, each 50c

No. 74. Shaving Paper Vases to match, each $1.15

Catalog reprint from *Barbers Supplies*, Theo Koch and Son, New York, catalog #15, 1915.

Imported Glassware—Original and Exclusive Designs

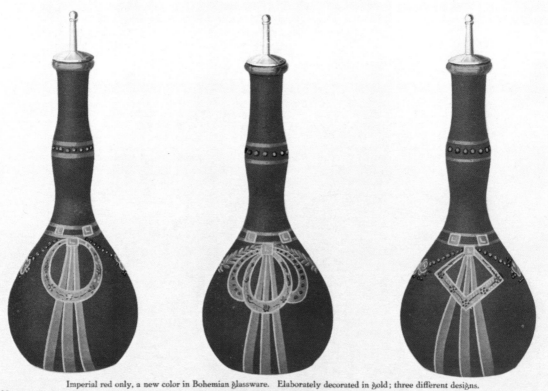

Made of clear glass treated in a manner so as to produce a frosted and glistening effect.   The different colored berries are raised.

No. 78.   Bottles, each.................................... 50c   No. 78.   Bowls to match, each.............................. 55c

No. 78.   Shaving Paper Vases to match, each..................... $1.25

Imperial red only, a new color in Bohemian glassware.   Elaborately decorated in gold; three different designs.

No. 76.   Bottles, each.................................... 90c   No. 76.   Bowls to match, each.............................. 95c

No. 76.   Shaving Paper Vases to match, each..................... $2.25

Catalog reprint from *Barbers Supplies*, Theo Koch and Son, New York, catalog #15, 1915.

Imported Glassware—Original and Exclusive Designs

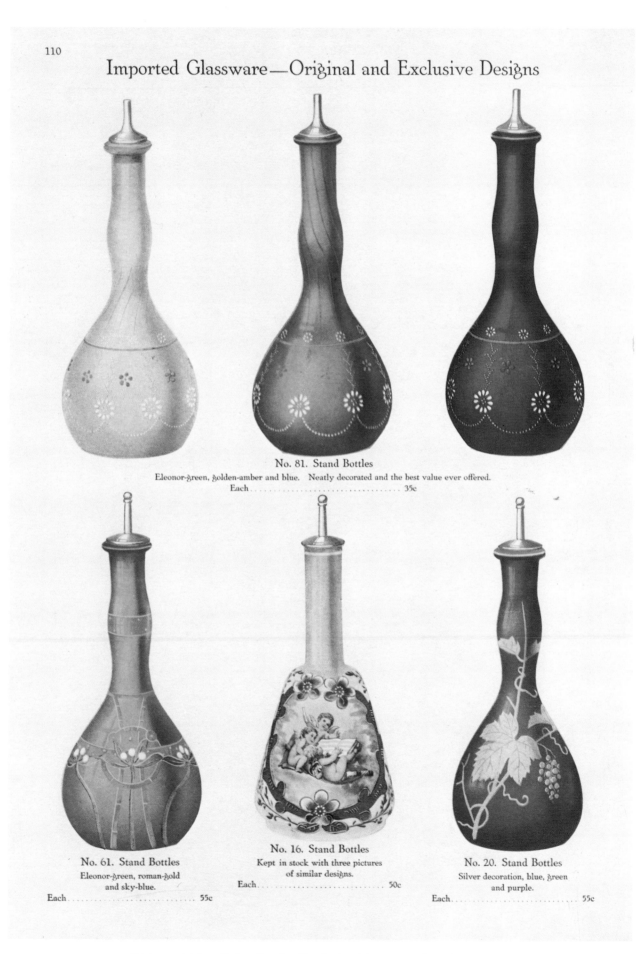

No. 81. Stand Bottles

Eleonor-green, golden-amber and blue.   Neatly decorated and the best value ever offered.

Each 35c

No. 61. Stand Bottles

Eleonor-green, roman-gold
and sky-blue.

Each 55c

No. 16. Stand Bottles

Kept in stock with three pictures
of similar designs.

Each 50c

No. 20. Stand Bottles

Silver decoration, blue, green
and purple.

Each 55c

Catalog reprint from *Barbers Supplies*, Theo Koch and Son, New York, catalog #15, 1915.

Imported Glassware—Original and Exclusive Designs

No. 75. Bohemian Glassware

Made of varicolored glass, producing a marbled effect which is very striking. Handsomely decorated in gold.

PRICES

No. 75. Stand Bottles, orange, rose and green, each......... 60c   No. 75. Bowls, each... 65c

No. 75. Shaving Paper Vases, 7 inches high, each................. $1.50

Catalog reprint from *Barbers Supplies*, Theo Koch and Son, New York, catalog #15, 1915.

112

Imported Glassware
Original and Exclusive Designs

No. 76. Bowl

Each 95c

No. 61. Bowl

Each 55c

No. 53. Bowl

Each 50c

No. 7. Antiseptic Vase
For holding sterilizing liquid for razors and tools.

Each $1.00

No. 25. Bowl

Each 35c

No. 74. Bowl

Each 50c

No. 8. Bowl

Each 50c

No. 24. Stand Bottles
Five inscriptions:
Bay Rum, Witch Hazel, Hair Tonic, Shampoo, Toilet Water.
Each 65c

No. 17
Brilliantine Bottle
Each 25c

No. 28. Stand Bottles
Each 55c

No. 26
Pomade Jar
Gilt cover
Each 25c

No. 8. Stand Bottles
Five inscriptions:
Bay Rum, Witch Hazel, Hair Tonic, Shampoo, Toilet Water.
Each 50c

Catalog reprint from *Barbers Supplies*, Theo Koch and Son, New York, catalog #15, 1915.

LETOURNEAUX
EAU DE QUININE HAIR TONIC

A Genuine Quinine Tonic
Prepared after the French Process

LETOURNEAUX EAU de QUININE HAIR TONIC enjoys immense popularity among barbers everywhere, and for some very good reasons. Letourneaux Eau de Quinine possesses the genuine odor of the French Tonic. It has full strength, containing 62% grain alcohol, and a rich color. It is sold to barbers only and at reasonable prices. It gives perfect satisfaction to the customers, and at the price received for each application, affords a good margin of profit. Letourneaux Eau de Quinine Hair Tonic is put up in sealed packages only.

This Colored Transfer Window Sign
Size 9¾ x 16 inches
Furnished Free. Ask for it.

This Sign
beautifully lithographed in colors,
Size 7¾ x 11
Furnished Free. Ask for it.

This Sign
beautifully lithographed in colors
Size 7½ x 11
Furnished Free. Ask for it.

Letourneaux
Eau de Quinine
8-ounce bottles.

This Stand Bottle
furnished free with orders
for Letourneaux
Eau de Quinine,

Letourneaux Eau de Quinine Hair Tonic

PRICES:

Per gallon	$4.50
Per half gallon	2.25
Per quart	1.15
Per pint	.60
Per dozen 8-ounce bottles	5.00

Catalog reprint from *Barbers Supplies*, Theo Koch and Son, New York, catalog #15, 1915.

Catalog reprint from *Barbers Supplies*, Theo Koch and Son, New York, catalog #15, 1915.

Shampoo Liquor—Castle Brand

This sign, heavily embossed and
executed in colors, is
furnished free.

As a Liquid Shampoo
CASTLE BRAND
is widely known among barbers for possessing full strength
and refined odor. Castle Brand Shampoo Liquor goes the
farthest; it requires only a small quantity to produce a
copious lather and it has extraordinary cleansing properties.

Five Odors:
Orange, Mint, Quinine, Pineapple, Pine Tar

This sign, heavily embossed and
executed in colors, is
furnished free.

8-Ounce Size.

Stand Bottles
furnished free.

Castle Brand Shampoo Liquor

PRICES:

Per gallon	$2.50
Per half-gallon	1.35
Per quart	.75
Per pint	.40
8-ounce bottles, per dozen	2.40
8-ounce bottles, each	.20
2-ounce bottles, per dozen	1.25

Catalog reprint from *Barbers Supplies*, Theo Koch and Son, New York, catalog #15, 1915.

CANEXIA RUB
A Splendid Cooling Lotion

Canexia Rub is the most invigorating and refreshing preparation ever offered for barbers' use. It has been found one of the best money-makers for the shop because customers appreciate the exhilarating properties of the preparation.

After shampoo or scalp massage, Canexia Rub is particularly recommended because of its cooling properties. Applied to the forehead and rubbed into the scalp it produces relief from itching and burning of the scalp and alleviates headache.

This Stand Bottle
Made of clear glass, with colored label burnt in, is furnished free with Canexia Rub.

Canexia Rub

Invigorating and refreshing. An ideal lotion for the head.

Canexia Rub

A splendid lotion for use in summer. Extraordinarily cooling.

PRICES:

Per gallon	$4.50	Per quart	$1.25
Per half-gallon	2.25	Per pint	.65
8-ounce bottles, per dozen	$5.00		

Catalog reprint from *Barbers Supplies*, Theo Koch and Son, New York, catalog #15, 1915.

List of References

The Antique Trader, February 27, 1973, "The Beauty of Barber Bottles" by James Matthews.

Collecting Bottles for Fun and Profit by William C. Ketchum Jr.

Armor's "Barbers Bought Better Bottles", *Old Bottle Magazine II,* March, 1969, by Dorothy McMillen.

Barber Bottles with Prices by Robert Namiat.

A Treasury of American Bottles by William C. Ketchum, Jr.

The Antiques Journal, October, 1965, "Those Beautiful Bottles Are Coming Back" by James Brescoll.

The Wooden Nutmeg, November, 1978, "A Shave and a Hair Cut — Victorian Style". An article done on a Connecticut bottle show, on the partial showing of Toney Gugliottis' collection of barber shop antiques, considered to be as fine as there is.

Price Guide

Page 7   Matched pair, iridescent green - $400.00-450.00 pr.

Page 8   Matched pair, cobalt blue - $400.00-450.00 pr.

Page 9   Matched pair, cobalt blue and amethyst - $350.00-400.00 pr.

Page 10   Opalized cranberry - $200.00-250.00; Amethyst - $250.00-300.00

Page 11   Matched pair, amethyst - $425.00-475.00 pr.

Page 12   Matched pair, amethyst - $425.00-475.00 pr.

Page 13   Matched pair, green - $375.00-425.00 pr.

Page 14   Limegreen - $175.00-225.00

Page 15   Matched pair, cobalt blue - $400.00-450.00 pr.

Page 16   Matched pair, cranberry - $400.00-450.00 pr.

Page 17   Three T. White Hall Tatum - $500.00+ each. One on left has name ground off, decreasing its value.

Page 18   Matched pair, hand painted milk glass - $250.00-300.00 pr.

Page 19   Seafoam - $150.00-200.00; Toilet Water - $125.00-175.00; Tonic or Facial Splash - $150.00-200.00; Bay Rum - $150.00-200.00

Page 20   Matched pair, hand painted milk glass - $350.00-400.00 pr.

Page 21   Blue milk glass - $150.00-200.00; hand painted milk glass - $125.00-175.00

Page 22   Top: Pair of dresser bottles - $50.00-75.00 (clear), $100.00-150.00 (white); Milk glass dresser bottle - $75.00-125.00; Koken Barber Supply bottle - $25.00-50.00; Bottom: Pair of white and black milk glass - $25.00-50.00 (white), $125.00-175.00 (black)

Page 23   Bristol glass - $150.00-200.00; milk glass - $125.00-175.00

Page 24   Blue mellon sided - $100.00-150.00; Koken Barber Supply - $25.00-50.00; French, cobalt blue - $175.00-225.00; Light blue with design - $75.00-125.00

Page 25   Matched pair, opalized cranberry splatter - $250.00-300.00 pr.

Page 26   Opalized cranberry splatter - $300.00-350.00; Opalized cranberry splatter - $175.00-225.00

Page 27   Opalized cranberry splatter - $150.00-200.00

Page 28   Opalized green splatter - $150.00-200.00

Page 29   Cranberry - $150.00-200.00

Page 30   Venetian glass - $175.00-225.00

Page 31   Blue and purple Art glass - $175.00-225.00

Page 32   Enameled and hand painted - $150.00-200.00

Page 33   Ruby cut to clear Bohemian style - $150.00-200.00

Page 34   Ruby cut to clear Bohemian style - $175.00-225.00

Page 35   Amethyst - $125.00-175.00

Page 36   Matched pair, amethyst - $200.00-250.00 pr.

Page 37   Matched pairs, (2) green, (2) amethyst - $200.00-250.00 pr.

Page 38   Cut crystal dresser bottle - $500.00+

Page 39   Frosted Stars and Stripes - $100.00-150.00; Fancy cut dresser bottle - $175.00-225.00

Page 40   Heavy crystal dresser bottle - $200.00-250.00; crystal, New England glass - $75.00-125.00

Page 41   Cut and etched dresser bottle - $175.00-225.00

Page 42   Top: Pressed star burst design - $50.00-75.00; Pressed diamond design - $75.00-100.00; Bottom: Matched set of fancy dresser bottles - $100.00-150.00

Page 43   Bristol glass dresser bottle - $75.00-125.00

Page 44   Pink Bristol glass dresser bottle - $75.00-125.00

Page 45   Aqua blue - $100.00-150.00; Ruby red - $175.00-200.00

Page 46   Left: Teal blue - $150.00-200.00; Right: Cobalt blue enameled miniature - $150.00-200.00

Page 47   Miniature brilliantine bottle - $125.00-175.00

Page 48   Teal blue mellon sided Coin Spot - $125.00-175.00; Bristol glass - $200.00-250.00

Page 49   Light amber - $175.00-225.00; Apple green - $125.00-175.00

Page 50   Pair, amethyst and light blue - $150.00-200.00 each

Page 51   Amethyst - $125.00-175.00

Page 52   Amethyst - $125.00-175.00

Page 53   Opalized cranberry - $125.00-175.00

Page 54   Iridescent amber - $200.00-250.00

Page 55   Amethyst - $250.00-300.00

Page 56   Matched pair, amethyst - $300.00-350.00 pr.

Page 57   Pair, light blue and cobalt blue - $125.00-175.00 each

Page 58   Amber - $125.00-175.00

Page 59   Multi-color Venetian glass - $125.00-175.00; Fenton Art glass - $125.00-175.00; very light blue - $125.00-150.00

Page 60   Amberina Hobnail - $150.00-200.00

Page 61   Pair, satin finish amethyst and opalized blue Hobnail - $150.00-175.00 (amethyst), $100.00-125.00 (blue)

Page 62   Matched pair, vaseline and light blue Hobnail - $200.00-250.00 pr.

Page 63   Pair, opalized blue Hobnail - $100.00-125.00 each

Page 64   Matched pair, amethyst - $250.00-300.00 pr.

Page 65   Matched pair, vaseline Hobnail - $200.00-250.00 pr.

Page 66   Matched pair, amber Hobnail - $200.00-250.00 pr.

Page 67   Matched pair, cranberry Hobnail - $225.00-275.00 pr.

Page 68   Pair, opalized cranberry Hobnail - $125.00-150.00 each

Page 69   Pair, clear opalized Hobnail - $100.00-125.00 each

Page 70   Matched pair, opalized yellow green - $200.00-250.00 pr.

Page 71   Pair, opalized cranberry mellon sided - $100.00-150.00 each

Page 72   Teal blue - $125.00-175.00; opalized cranberry - $100.00-150.00

Page 73   Limegreen - $125.00-175.00; Cobalt blue - $125.00-150.00

Page 74   Opalized cranberry - $150.00-200.00; Emerald green - $125.00-150.00

Page 75   Matched pair, opalized cranberry Coin Spot - $250.00-300.00 pr.

Page 76   Opalized blue "Stars and Stripes" - $125.00-175.00

Page 77   Opalized blue Spanish Lace - $125.00-175.00; Opalized cranberry swirl - $125.00-275.00

Page 78   Opalized pale green - $100.0-150.00; Opalized cranberry - $125.00-175.00

Page 79   Matched set, mellon sided cranberry - $150.00-200.00 pr.; Matched set, Thumb Print cranberry - $150.00-200.00 pr.

Page 80   Matched pair, clear opalized Coin Spot - $200.00-250.00 pr.

Page 81   Cobalt blue - $100.00-125.00; light blue - $100.00-150.00

Page 82   Pair, opalized blue and cranberry Spanish Lace - $125.00-175.00 each

Page 83   Pair, opalized clear and cranberry swirl - $125.00-175.00 each

Page 84   Matched pair, amethyst and cobalt blue - $250.00-300.00 pr.

Page 85   Pair, dark and emerald green - $125.00-175.00 each

Page 86   Pair, amethyst and light blue - $100.00-150.00 each

Page 87   Pair, amethyst - $125.00-175.00 each

Page 88   Pair, amethyst and green - $250.00-300.00 pr.

Page 89   Matched pair, light blue and amethyst - $200.00-250.00 pr.

Page 90   Pair, Bristol glass - $75.00-100.00 each

Page 91   Green glass in wicker - $75.00-100.00

Page 92   Close Harmony - under $30.00

Page 93   Pair, cased satin glass pink and yellow - $50.00-75.00

Page 94   Porcelain with overlay - $75.00-100.00; Cobalt blue with design - $100.00-125.00; Bristol glass - $25.00-50.00

Page 95   Bristol glass - $100.00-125.00; Opalized cranberry swirl - $125.00-175.00

Page 96   Matched pair, opaline - $100.00-150.00 pr.

Page 97   Top; Set, opaline - $150.00-200.00 set; Bottom: Set, opaline - $125.00-175.00 set

Page 98   Set, opaline - $100.00-150.00 set

Page 99   Set, three Wapler Barber Supply House bottles - $50.0-75.00 each

Page 100   Group of commercial bottles - under $40.00

Page 101   Matched pair, label unde glass overlay - $200.00-250.00 pr.

Page 102   Hair Tonic bottle - under $40.00

Page 103   Pair, Ayer's Hair Vigor bottle - $25.00-75.00

Page 104   Colgate Commercial Toilet Water - under $20.00; Palmer Commercial Toilet Water - $50.00-75.00; Kickapoo Sage Commercial Hair Tonic - $25.00-50.00; Demond Brand Commercial Hair Oil - under $20.00

Page 105   Pair, facial splash bottles - (green) under $35.00, (amber) under $20.00

Page 106   Bay Rum bottles - under $20.00

Page 107   Sprosmans Shaving Lotion - $25.00+; Amber - under $50.00; T. White Hall Tatum Bay Rum - under $25.00

Page 108   Pair, clear pressed - $25.00-50.00

Page 109   Group of clear pressed glass - under $20.00

Page 110   Group of clear pressed glass - under $25.00

Page 111   Group of Bitters bottles - under $25.00

Page 112   Group of supply house bottles - under $25.00

Page 113   Matched pair, T. White Hall Tatum milk glass - 1000.00 pair; Bottom: Clear glass with label - $100.00-125.00

Page 114   Clear opalized Hobnail - $75.00-100.00; Hand painted milk glass - $125.00-175.00; Milk glass - $50.00-75.00; Clear opalized Stars & Stripes - $125.00-175.00

Page 115   Matched pair, Art glass - $400.00-450.00; Emerald green toilet water - under $50.00; cobalt blue - $250.00-300.00; Pressed, ruby flash - $100.00-150.00

Two Important Tools For The
Astute Antique Dealer, Collector and Investor

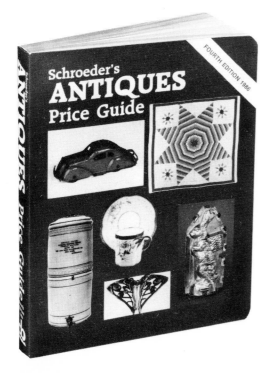

Schroeder's Antiques Price Guide

The very best low cost investment that you can make if you are really serious about antiques and collectibles is a good identification and price guide. We publish and highly recommend **Schroeder's Antiques Price Guide.** Our editors and writers are very careful to seek out and report accurate values each year. We do not simply change the values of the items each year but start anew to bring you an entirely new edition. If there are repeats, they are by chance and not by choice. Each huge edition (it weighs 3 pounds!) has over 56,000 descriptions and current values on 608 - 8½x11 pages. There are hundreds and hundreds of categories and even more illustrations. Each topic is introduced by an interesting discussion that is an education in itself. Again, no dealer, collector or investor can afford not to own this book. It is available from your favorite bookseller or antiques dealer at the low price of $9.95. If you are unable to find this price guide in your area, it's available from Collector Books, P. O. Box 3009, Paducah, KY 42001 at $9.95 plus $1.00 for postage and handling.

Flea Market Trader

Bargains are pretty hard to come by these days -- especially in the field of antiques and collectibles, and everyone knows that the most promising sources for those seldom-found under-priced treasures are flea markets. To help you recognize a bargain when you find it, you'll want a copy of the *Flea Market Trader* --the only price guide on the market that deals exclusively with all types of merchandise you'll be likely to encounter in the marketplace. It contains not only reliable pricing information, but the *Flea Market Trader* will be the first to tune you in to the market's newest collectible interests -- you will be able to buy before the market becomes established, before prices have a chance to excalate! You'll not only have the satisfaction of being first in the know, but you'll see your investments appreciate dramatically. You will love the format. Its handy 5½" x 8½" size will tuck easily into pocket or purse. Its common sense organization along with detailed index makes finding your subject a breeze. There's tons of information and hundreds of photos to aid in identification. It's written with first-hand insight and an understanding of market activities. It's reliable, informative, comprehensive; it's a bargain! From Collector Books, P.O. Box 3009 Paducah, Kentucky 42001. $8.95 plus $1.00 postage and handling.